HOW TO

Sleep
Tight

THROUGH THE NIGHT

HOW TO
Sleep
Tight

THROUGH THE NIGHT

Bedtime Tricks
(That Really Work!) for Kids

Tzivia Gover & **Lesléa Newman**

Illustrated by Vivian Mineker

Storey Publishing

The mission of Storey Publishing is to serve our customers by
publishing practical information that encourages
personal independence in harmony with the environment.

Edited by Deanna F. Cook and Sarah Guare
Art direction and book design by Carolyn Eckert
Text production by Liseann Karandisecky
Illustrations by © Vivian Mineker

Text © 2022 by Tzivia Gover and Lesléa Newman

Storey Publishing
210 MASS MoCA Way
North Adams, MA 01247
storey.com

Printed in China by Toppan Leefung Printing Ltd.
10 9 8 7 6 5 4 3 2 1

Library of Congress Cataloging-in-Publication Data on file

For children everywhere—sleep tight!

Let's Go to Sleep!

Some nights, you just don't want to shut out the lights—or shut your eyes—at bedtime because there are still fun things to do.

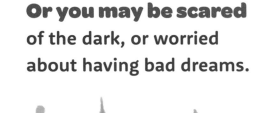

Or you may be scared of the dark, or worried about having bad dreams.

But you need sleep, even more than grown-ups do. And you need more of it! That's because while you sleep, your body and brain are busy helping you grow. Plus, when you get a good night's sleep, you feel sunnier and more energetic when you wake up.

Luckily, you can get better at sleep, just as you can get better at throwing a ball or playing an instrument. It just takes practice.

Feel good and cozy at bedtime, fall asleep, and become friends with your dreams by following the suggestions in this book. So, turn the page. Before you know it, you'll be ready to turn over and turn off the light.

Make a Night Notebook

Keep a notebook by your bed. You can buy a notebook or make your own by folding and stapling or sewing several pieces of paper together. Use stickers, markers, or crayons to decorate the cover.

On the cover, draw a picture of your favorite stuffed toy, the stars and moon, or an animal friend to help you feel safe and cozy when you pick it up to write or draw.

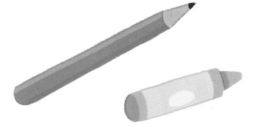

Before you go to sleep, draw or write about your day.

After you wake up, draw or write about your dreams.

Love Your Bed

Some kids can fall asleep in the back seat of the car, or on the couch, but there's one place that's meant just for sleeping: your bed! Sure, you do other things in your room besides sleep, but it's called a bedroom because sleeping in your bed is the most important thing to do there.

What do you love about your bed?

My animals who sleep with me

My special pillow

My cozy blanket

Draw a picture
of your cozy bed
before you snuggle
in and get sleepy!

Swap Plugs for Pages

The hour before bedtime, or after you get into your pajamas, is the time to unplug your electronics.

Trading plugs for pages helps your brain slow down so you can recharge overnight and power up for a new day.

Instead of watching TV or going online, read a book.

Instead of playing a video game, do a puzzle or play a board game.

Add Pizzazz to Your Pillow

Here's a fun way to slip into dreams. Ask a grown-up for a plain pillowcase and permission to decorate it. Find some fabric markers and a piece of cardboard, then let's get started.

* Choose what you want to draw. Think of something that makes you smile: stars, the moon, your favorite animal, or a picture from a dream!

* Practice drawing it on paper.

* Next, place a piece of cardboard inside the pillowcase, so the colors don't run through.

* Using fabric markers, draw your creation on the pillowcase.

* Let the ink dry overnight. Take out the cardboard and wash the pillowcase before putting it on your pillow.

Follow the Milky Way

There are lots of things to do before going to bed, like tidying your room, brushing your teeth, and changing into your pajamas. Those things might seem boring because you do them every night. But there's a fun way to think about your bedtime routine.

Did you know there's **a starry path** through the night sky **called the Milky Way?**

Imagine that as you take each step to get ready for bed, you are **stepping from star to star** on a path that leads into the land of sleep.

17

Three (or More!) Good Reasons to Go to Bed

It's bedtime, but you want to keep playing. Instead of coming up with reasons why you should stay awake, think of three (or more) reasons why it's really a good idea to go to bed. For example:

1. While you sleep, your body works hard to grow.

2. When you sleep, your brain helps you remember what you learned during the day.

3. Your dreams have a job to do, too. They help you feel calmer and happier.

My stuffies miss me when I'm not in bed!

What are three more— serious or silly— reasons to go to bed?

My hair needs time to grow.

19

Make Sweet-Smelling Dreams!

The smell of some flowers and plants can relax you. Others help you have more dreams, or better dreams. Mix them up and you can make a dream sock to put under your pillow.

Grab a handful each of three or four of these dried herbs:

mugwort or **rose petals** for dreams that might come true

jasmine or **rosemary** for good dreams

Mix the herbs together.

lavender to help you relax

Spoon the herbs into a clean sock. Stuff it loosely.

Tie the top of the sock with a tight knot.

For extra softness, add cotton balls in the toe of the sock and on top of the herbs.

Sweet dreams

Slip your sock under your pillow or into your pillowcase.

Pitch a Reading Tent

Find a flashlight and gather up your favorite stuffed animal and a book. Crawl into bed and pull the covers up over your head, so you feel like you're inside a tent.

Read in your cozy hiding place for a few minutes, then shut off the flashlight and go to sleep.

Say Thank You

Some people count sheep to fall asleep. But counting the things you feel grateful for works even better. Before bed, make a list or draw pictures of things that made you feel good today. Then, when you're tucked under the covers, close your eyes, imagine each one, and silently say thank you.

Let yourself drift off to sleep with a smile.

Thank you, nature.

Thank you, ice cream.

Thank you, friends.

Thank you,
Grandpa.

Tuck Your Worries in at Night

Everyone worries sometimes. But worrying doesn't fix problems, and it just might keep you awake when you want to sleep.

If something is worrying you, **write it down on a slip of paper** and put it in a small container or box.

You can even decorate the box!

Imagine that a dream helper or fairy is taking care of your worries until morning.

So, instead of worrying, you can get a good night's sleep.

Watch the Stars Fall

Gazing up at the stars in the night sky can make you feel relaxed and sleepy. Whether or not you can see stars outside, you can bring them indoors with this project.

Make sure your jar has a lid that fits tightly.

1. Fill a glass jar one-third of the way full with very warm tap water. Add 1 to 3 drops of dark blue food coloring.

2. Add clear school glue until the jar is half full. Whisk until the glue dissolves.

3. Stir in a couple of spoonfuls of glitter (star glitter if you have it!).

4. Fill the jar to the top with more tap water.

5. Put the lid on and twist it until the jar is securely closed.

water + glitter

clear school glue

water + food coloring

GLUE

Before bed, shake the jar, then watch the stars

drift to the bottom as your thoughts settle down, too.

Climb aboard a Sleep Adventure

Bedtime doesn't have to be boring. When you close your eyes, imagine you are about to take a journey to dreamland. Snuggle under your favorite blanket, then . . .

Pretend your bed is flying through the sky.

Imagine it's a raft
that's floating down
a river.

Make believe
it's a magic train
chugging along
its tracks.

Climb aboard,
close your eyes, and
see where your
adventure leads you.

Nod Off with Numbers

If you want to sleep but your brain keeps spinning like a top, give your mind some numbers to focus on so you can sink into sleep.

Try counting backward from 10.

If any other thoughts come into your mind, just go back to 10 and try again.

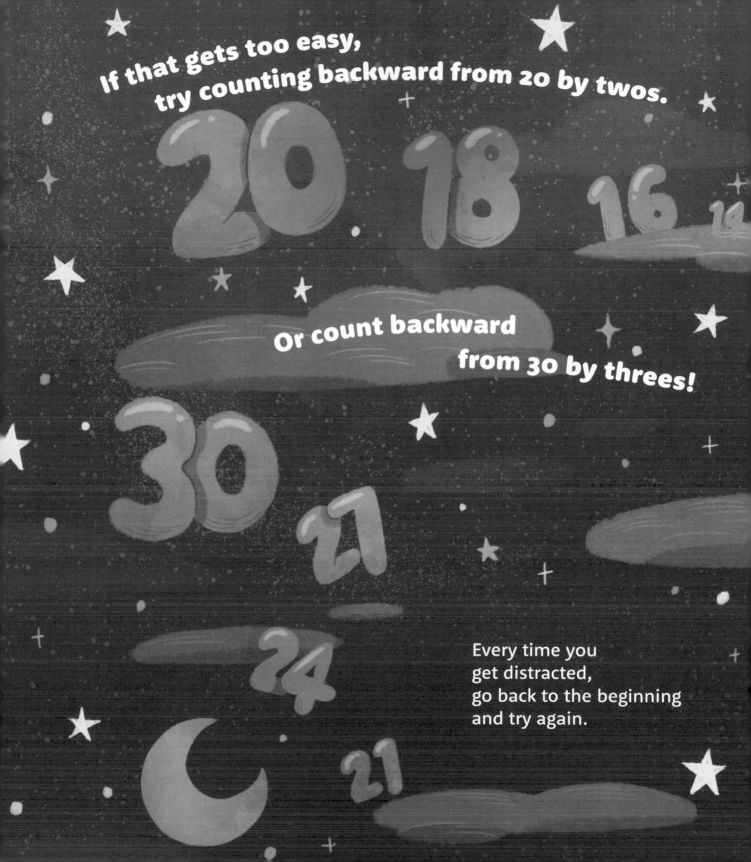

If that gets too easy, try counting backward from 20 by twos.

20 18 16 14

Or count backward from 30 by threes!

30 27 24 21

Every time you get distracted, go back to the beginning and try again.

Dream Power

Do you ever wish you could fly? In dreams you can do this and many other things!

What could you do in a dream that you can't do when you're awake?

Breathe In, Breathe Out

At bedtime, if you feel fidgety and can't settle down, try this.

Take a big breath in slowly, and silently say to yourself, "I am . . ."

Then breathe out even more slowly, and silently say, "sleepy!"

Slow your words and breath to a turtle's pace and keep going until you fall asleep.

Make a Wish

Wishing on birthday candles is fun, but birthdays only happen once a year. Luckily, there are lots of other times to make wishes, and bedtime is one of them.

Write a wish on a strip of paper

Become a dancer!

Swim with dolphins!

Drive trucks!

and put it under your pillow.

Think of anything you want!

In the morning, watch for
any small or big ways that your
wish might be coming true.

Think of Words from A to Zzzzz . . .

While you're lying in bed, think of as many words as you can that begin with the letter A. There's apple, aardvark, anteater, and abracadabra!

What else? Next, think of as many words as you can that begin with the letter B. Keep going through the alphabet.

Before you know it, you'll have gone from **A** to **Z**zzzz and be snoozing away!

Doze Off to Your Dream Movie

When you climb into bed, imagine you are entering an enchanted movie theater. You buy a ticket, but you have no idea what movie you are going to see.

Snuggle in under the covers and close your eyes.

Imagine a curtain opening up to reveal a magical screen.

Then wait for your dream movie to begin.

NOW PLAYING

Sleepwalk **in Your Head**

If it's hard to find your way to sleep, imagine walking your dog down the block, or walking to a friend's house close by. Picture how you would get there, step by step.

Close your eyes and imagine you are walking down your sidewalk.

Along the way, you might just wander off to sleep!

Scared? Call on Your Superpowers!

Everyone gets scared sometimes. But everyone has superpowers, too. You don't need an invisibility cloak and you don't have to fly through the clouds.
You have other strengths to help you face your fears.

What superpowers do you have to face your fears?

When you feel afraid of the dark, or if you wake in the night from a scary dream, think of your superpower to help you feel brave when you go back to sleep.

Sing a Sleep Song

The rhythm of a lullaby can rock you to sleep. If no one can sing to you before bed, you can make up your own song.

Put new words to your favorite lullaby:

Sleepy, sleepy little star,

I wonder what your sweet dreams are.

Up above the world so bright,

will you dream of me tonight?

Sleepy, sleepy little star,

I wonder what your sweet dreams are.

Or make up a song with the names of all the people who love you in it.

Or sing about the things that you're looking forward to seeing or doing tomorrow.

Sweet Dreams Jar

What are some things you want to dream about?
Write your ideas on small pieces of colorful paper
and place them in a glass jar.

Decorate the lid of the jar however you'd like!

As your jar fills up, it will get more and more colorful.

underwater adventures

skating day

see a sloth

Before you go to bed,
pick out a slip of paper.

Happy dreaming!

Did any of your ideas appear in your dreams?

Read Your Dreams

Sometimes it's hard to understand dreams. That's because dreams speak a special language that uses pictures instead of just words.

What might your dreams mean?

A bird might mean . . .

you feel as free as a bird.

A rainy day might mean . . .

you feel sad.

A rainbow might mean . . .

you feel happy.

A hissing cat might mean . . .

you feel angry.

A big wave overhead might mean . . .

you feel afraid.

Being lost in the woods might mean . . .

you feel lonely.

Have fun and remember, the only "right" way to read your dreams is the way that feels right to you.

Banish Bad Dreams by Calling out Colors

Everyone has bad dreams sometimes. If you wake up from a nightmare and feel scared, open your eyes and look around your room. What do you see?

"There's my red lamp."

Whisper the name of each familiar thing you see, along with its color.

"There's my pink poster."

"There's my purple bunny."

Soon you'll realize that you are safe at home in your very own bed and there's no need to feel afraid anymore.

Feel Better

Dreams bring up lots of different feelings. But they can be hard to describe. The following four emotions can help describe almost any feeling.

When you wake up from a dream, ask yourself:

Did I feel scared?

Did I feel mad?

**Naming your emotions
helps you talk about what's happening inside you,
so you can feel better.**

Did I feel sad?

Did I feel glad?

Make Friends with Monsters

If a mean dog or creepy ghost shows up in your dream, imagine you can shrink it until it fits inside a safe, clear box you can hold in your hand.

Now that it can't hurt you, ask it questions.

What's your name?

What do you want?

What do you need to tell me?

What are you afraid of?

Why are you scaring me?

Introduce your monster to a grown-up, too. Once you get to know this visitor, you'll start to feel stronger and less afraid.

Be a Sleep Scientist

Did you know that almost all animals dream? Scientists study people and animals while they sleep to learn about their dreams and how they sleep. You can, too.

Watch your pet while they sleep.
(If you don't have a pet, you may be able to watch a friend's pet.)

Do their eyelids twitch?

They might be dreaming.

Do they wag their tail?

Do they purr?

What else can you observe?
Write it down or draw a picture of what you see.

61

Yawn Big

Yawning doesn't always mean you're tired or bored. A great big yawn in the morning brings oxygen to your brain to help you get ready for the day. Add a stretch when you yawn and wake up your body, too.

Sit tall in bed or stand up.

Place your hands in front of your chest with your elbows sticking out like chicken wings.

Take a big breath and fill your body with air.

Open your arms wide, open your mouth, stretch, and let out a great big yawn!

YAAAWWNN

YAAWWNN

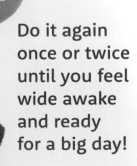

Do it again once or twice until you feel wide awake and ready for a big day!